CONTEMPORARY'S
LET'S READ TOGETHER

Safe at Home

Clairece Feagin

Project Editor
Sarah Conroy

Consultants
The Students and Staff
at the
National Center for Family Literacy
Louisville, KY

Meta Potts
Director of Adult Learning Services

Bonnie Lash Freeman
Director of Early Childhood Services

Field-testers
Mary Jo Brown

Marjorie Spearman

Jennifer Whitehead

D0169980

CB

CONTEMPORARY
BOOKS

CHICAGO

Library of Congress Cataloging-in-Publication Data

Feagin, Clairece Booher.
    Safe at home. Book 3 / Clairece Feagin.
        p.   cm.—(Let's read together)
    Summary: Describes techniques of fire prevention such as fire
drills and fire inspections by means of a story about Roberto,
Sylvia, and their families and classmates.
    ISBN 0-8092-4012-2
    1. Fire prevention—Juvenile literature.   [1. Fire
prevention.   2. Safety.]   I. Title.   II. Series: Let's read
together (Chicago, Ill.)
    TH9148.F43   1991
    628.9′2—dc20   91-12015
                                                                              CIP
                                                                               AC

Published by Contemporary Books, Inc.
180 North Michigan Avenue, Chicago, Illinois 60601
Manufactured in the United States of America
International Standard Book Number: 0-8092-4012-2

Published simultaneously in Canada by
Fitzhenry & Whiteside
195 Allstate Parkway
Valleywood Business Park
Markham, Ontario L3R 4T8
Canada

Editorial Director Caren Van Slyke	*Cover Design* Lois Stein
Editorial Cathy Hobbins Erica Pochis Chris Benton Cyndy Raucci	*Cover Illustrator* Quang Ho *Cover Inset Illustrator* Kathy Petrauskas
Editorial Production Manager Norma Fioretti	*Interior Illustrator* Linda Reilly
Production Editor Marina Micari	*Art & Production* Jan Geist

CHILD'S STORY

Contents

Characters

Roberto Gonzales, age 6

Mrs. Gonzales

Sylvia Lozano, age 6

Mr. Lozano

Mrs. Green, a neighbor

Turn the book over to read a story
just for parents.

A fire drill can help keep you safe. Do you
know what a fire drill is?

Chapter 1   What's a Fire Drill?

"Safe!" Roberto shouted as he ran into his apartment. His friend Sylvia came running up the stairs right behind him.

"Are you kids playing chase again?" Mrs. Gonzalez asked her son.

"Yeah. But she can't catch me. I run *fast!*" Roberto said.

"How was school?" his mother asked. "What did you do today?"

"We read a new story," Roberto told her. "And the teacher said we're going to have a fire drill this week. What's a fire drill?"

"A fire drill is practice. You practice what to do in case there's a fire," Mrs. Gonzalez said.

"I know what to do!" Sylvia pretended to squirt water with a big fire hose. "I'm going to be a fire fighter just like my dad."

"A fire drill isn't for putting out a fire," Mrs. Gonzalez told the children. "It's for you to learn how to get out of the school quickly. The fire bell rings. Then all the teachers and children go outside."

"I'll be the first one out. I can run fast," Roberto said.

"You shouldn't run in a fire drill," Mrs. Gonzalez said. "You might knock someone down."

Have you ever had a fire drill at your school? Why is it important for children not to run in a fire drill?

"Does a fire drill mean that there's a fire?" Roberto asked.

"No. A fire drill is only for practice. You learn what to do in a fire drill. Then you will know what to do if there's ever a real fire," Mrs. Gonzalez told him.

"Will there be a real fire at school?" Roberto asked.

"I hope not," Mrs. Gonzalez said.

"I'm going to ask my dad if we can have a fire drill here in our building," Sylvia said. "That would be fun."

"Why do we need to have a fire drill here?" Roberto asked.

"Apartment buildings can have fires, too," Mrs. Gonzalez said.

"Yeah, like the building over on Second Street," Sylvia said. "My dad helped put out that fire."

"Will that ever happen to our building?" Roberto asked.

"I hope not," Mrs. Gonzalez said. "But if a fire got started in our building, we would have to go outside right away."

"Could we get all our stuff out before it burned?" Roberto asked.

"No," Mrs. Gonzalez told him. "When a fire starts, you have to get the people out first. Fire spreads quickly."

"But what about my toys? And all our other stuff?" Roberto asked.

"It's better to lose things than for anyone to get hurt," Mrs. Gonzalez said. "But it's best not to have a fire at all."

Chapter 2   How Do Fires Start?

"How do fires start?" Roberto asked.

"My dad said the fire on Second Street started with someone smoking in bed," Sylvia said. "They fell asleep. The cigarette set the bed on fire."

"A lot of fires start in the kitchen," Mrs. Gonzalez said. "What do you see here in our kitchen that could burn easily?" she asked.

"The oven might get too hot," Sylvia said.

"Yeah. Or the coffeepot could blow up!" Roberto added.

"Look at the dish towel. And the pot holder. If they touch the burner on the stove, they can catch on fire," Mrs. Gonzalez said.

"Even that box of rice?" asked Roberto.

"Yes," Mrs. Gonzalez agreed. "And sometimes, food cooking in a pan can catch on fire if it gets too hot."

"I'm not allowed to do anything in the kitchen unless my mom or my dad's there," Sylvia said.

"We have the same rule here," Mrs. Gonzalez told her. "Children should always have an adult with them when they cook things in the kitchen."

Look around your kitchen. How many things do you see that could burn easily?

Chapter 3   Sylvia's Dad Arrives

Just then someone knocked on the apartment door. Mrs. Gonzalez opened the door. There stood Mr. Lozano, Sylvia's dad.

"I came by to see if you had an extra kid!" Mr. Lozano smiled.

"Dad!" Sylvia shouted. "Can we have a fire drill? I mean, here in our building."

"A fire drill?" Mr. Lozano asked. "What made you think of a fire drill?"

"We're having a fire drill at school. I want to have one here, too."

"Sounds like a good idea to me," Mr. Lozano said.

"We were just talking about how fires start," Mrs. Gonzalez said.

"Yeah. Like when people drop cigarettes or matches. Or when things touch the burner on the stove," Roberto said.

"Accidents like that cause lots of fires," Mr. Lozano said. "I have an idea," he added. "Would you kids like to help me do a fire safety check of this building? We could do it Saturday morning. I'll show you more ways that fires get started. And we can look for ways to make the building safer."

"I want to," Roberto said eagerly. "Is it OK, Mom?"

"I think that's a great idea," Mrs. Gonzalez said.

Do you think it's a good idea to have a fire drill in an apartment building?

Chapter 4   Fire Safety Check

On Saturday morning, Roberto was up early. After breakfast, he ran upstairs to the Lozanos' apartment and knocked on the door. Mr. Lozano was just finishing his coffee.

"I'm glad to have such eager helpers," he told the children.

"What are we going to do?" asked Roberto.

"Well, there are six apartments in this building. I've asked all the neighbors if we can check their apartments. We'll see how safe each apartment is," Mr. Lozano said.

"I've made a list of things we should look for. And we can also tell everyone about the fire drill," he added.

"When will we have the fire drill?" Sylvia asked.

"Today!" Roberto said. "Let's have it today."

"We can have it later this afternoon," Mr. Lozano said. "We can ring this big bell to let people know it's time to leave the building."

Roberto picked up the bell and rang it.

"Everyone in town can hear this bell," Roberto said.

"Can we show the bell to everyone when we check their apartments?" Sylvia asked.

"Good idea," Mr. Lozano said. "Are we all ready? Why don't we start with Mrs. Green on the first floor?" he suggested. "She's always up early."

Mrs. Green's Apartment

Roberto didn't know Mrs. Green very well. She was kind and friendly, but he didn't see her very often. She was old and didn't go out a lot.

The children ran down the stairs ahead of Mr. Lozano. They knocked on Mrs. Green's door.

"We're here for the fire safety check," they told her. "Are you ready?"

"Good morning, children," Mrs. Green said. "Well, I suppose I'm ready. I hope my home is safe. I don't move around as fast as I used to. If I had a fire, I don't know if I'd get out in time!"

"Good morning, Mrs. Green," Mr. Lozano said. "Thanks for agreeing to the safety check. We're looking for things that could start a fire, and for things that make fire spread fast."

"Well, I hope I don't have anything here that will start a fire," Mrs. Green said. "I don't smoke. My stove is electric. And I put a new battery in my smoke detector last week."

"If you drop your dish towel or pot holder on your stove when it's hot, that could start a fire, you know," Sylvia said.

"That's right, dear," Mrs. Green said. "I try to be careful about that."

"Look at this frayed cord," Mr. Lozano said. "When the cords of electric appliances get old and frayed, they can cause fires."

"My son promised to fix that soon," Mrs. Green told him.

"Well, it needs to be repaired right away. If your son doesn't have time, I'll fix it for you," Mr. Lozano said.

"That's a big pile of newspapers!" said Sylvia.

"Sylvia's right," Mr. Lozano said. "Are you keeping these for anything special?"

"Not really," Mrs. Green said.

"Stacks of paper like this are a fire hazard," Mr. Lozano told her. "You really need to get rid of these. The city sends a truck around every week. It picks up papers to recycle. Maybe you can get someone to carry these papers out for you."

"We can carry them out," Roberto said.

"Sure," Sylvia said. "We can come get them after we finish our safety check."

"Once that cord is fixed and you get those papers out, your apartment will be in good shape," Mr. Lozano told her.

"We're going to have a fire drill in our building," Sylvia told Mrs. Green.

"A fire drill!" Mrs. Green said. "It's been a long time since I was in a fire drill. I can't get out of the building as fast as I used to, you know."

"I'll stop by your place during the fire drill. I'll see if you need any help," Mr. Lozano said.

Do you know any people in your neighborhood who might need help keeping their homes safe?

Chapter 5   Danger in the Basement

Roberto, Sylvia, and Mr. Lozano visited all the apartments in their building. When Sylvia saw people smoking, she told them to be careful. She told them not to let their cigarettes set the bed or the couch on fire.

Roberto looked for stacks of old newspapers and offered to help carry them out.

In one kitchen, Roberto saw a box of matches. The matches sat near the burner of the gas stove.

"Those matches could catch on fire when you're cooking on that burner," he said.

"Very good, Roberto," Mr. Lozano told him. "You're a first-rate inspector!"

The children told their neighbors in every apartment about the fire drill.

After all the apartments had been checked, Mr. Lozano and the children went down to the basement. They found something there that made Mr. Lozano very worried.

"I wonder who left these dirty rags here by the furnace," Mr. Lozano said.

"They've got paint on them," Roberto said.

"These dirty rags can catch on fire very easily," Mr. Lozano told the children. "When the weather gets cold, and we turn on the furnace, these rags could set the whole building on fire. Dirty rags are a fire hazard anywhere. But they are really dangerous near a furnace," he added.

"What can we do with these dirty rags?" Roberto asked.

"To throw these away safely, we need a metal container. Something airtight, like an empty coffee can with a lid. If air can't touch these rags, they won't catch on fire," Mr. Lozano said.

Roberto raced up the stairs to his own apartment.

"Mom!" he shouted. "I need an empty coffee can. We found a pile of dirty rags in the basement. Mr. Lozano said they could set the whole building on fire. He's going to put them in the metal can to throw them away."

"Will this one do?" Mrs. Gonzalez asked. She gave Roberto a large empty coffee can.

"Thanks, Mom," Roberto said as he ran back to the basement.

Do a fire safety check of your own home. Help your parents:

- carry out piles of newspapers
- safely throw away dirty rags
- watch out for frayed cords
- check the smoke detectors in your home every month

Chapter 6   The Fire Drill

"Is it time for the fire drill yet?" Sylvia asked when her family finished eating lunch.

"I've got a few things to do," her dad told her. "Let's have the fire drill at four o'clock. That should give you and Roberto time to carry out Mrs. Green's papers."

Roberto and Sylvia finished carrying the papers out. "Is it time yet?" Roberto asked Mr. Lozano.

"I'm ready if you are," Mr. Lozano said.

"Can I ring the bell?" Sylvia asked.

"Yes," Mr. Lozano said. "And Roberto can time the drill," he added, handing Roberto his watch.

Roberto was very excited. He held Mr. Lozano's watch carefully. The three of them walked downstairs and stood in front of the apartment building. Then Sylvia began to ring the bell. Roberto looked at the watch.

"Four o'clock," he said.

"Fire drill! Fire drill!" Roberto and Sylvia shouted.

Then people started coming through the front door. They walked halfway down the block. They stopped at the old tree, which Mr. Lozano had chosen as a safe meeting place.

Mr. Lozano went back in to Mrs. Green's apartment to see if she needed any help. Soon everyone was standing on the sidewalk next to the old tree.

"Is everyone here?" Mr. Lozano asked, looking through the crowd. "What time is it now, Roberto?" he asked.

"Three minutes after four," Roberto said.

"Everyone got out of the building very fast," Mr. Lozano said. "You used the exit we planned. No one ran. That's important in a real fire.

"If this were a real fire, the first one outside would go to the corner store to call the fire department. Remember, *first* leave the building. *Then* call the fire department from down the street," he said.

"You kids have done a good job," Mr. Lozano said proudly. "Thanks to you, we have a safer building now. And everyone knows how to get out quickly just in case we ever do have a fire."

Think about the Story

1. Have you ever been in a fire drill? How was it like or different from the one in this story?

2. Have you ever seen a building that has had a fire? What did it look like?
Draw a picture of it.

3. What are some ways that fires can start?
Make a list of as many as you can think of.

4. How can you make your home safer from fires?
Talk with your parents about your ideas.

5. If you are in a building and a fire starts, what should you do? Why?

Ideas from the Story

Children can help prevent fires. Here are some safety tips.

- Never play with matches.
- Never use the stove without an adult in the kitchen.
- Don't keep old papers or dirty rags around.
- Tell your parents if you see an electric cord that is broken or damaged.

If you are ever in a building and a fire starts, it is important to get out of the building quickly. Don't panic. Don't run or push other people. Just walk quickly to the nearest outside door and away from the building. Go to a house or store nearby to call the fire department.

End of Child's Story

Turn the book over to read a story
just for parents.

PARENT'S STORY

Contents

Characters

Maria Gonzales

Tony Gonzales, age 2

Josie Lozano, Maria's neighbor

Marge, an emergency medical worker

Steve, an emergency medical worker

Dr. Williams

Rosa, the hospital social worker

Turn the book over to read a story
for parents and children.

Many children are hurt in accidents at home every day. What are some ways parents can keep children safe at home?

Chapter 1   Tony's Accident

Maria Gonzalez was busy in the kitchen when she heard Tony waking up from his nap. Tony had been sick with a bad cold. Maria hoped he would be feeling better after his nap.

Maria lifted Tony in her arms.

"You look like you're feeling better," she said as she hugged him. "Would you like a cookie?" she asked.

Just then the phone rang. Maria carried Tony into the living room and picked up the phone.

"Hello," she said. "Oh, Nita! I'm glad you called. Your party is Saturday, right?"

Maria sat down. She and Nita had a lot to talk about. Tony sat quietly on his mother's lap for a bit. Then he began to wiggle around. He slid down.

"I'll be off the phone in a minute," Maria whispered to Tony.

But Tony was hungry. He wanted a cookie now. While his mother talked on the phone, Tony went into the kitchen to look for the cookies.

Something was cooking in a pot on the stove. It smelled good to Tony. He reached up and put his hand on the handle of the pot. He stood on his tiptoes to see what was in the pot. But Tony pulled too hard on the pot's handle, and suddenly hot soup spilled all over him.

Maria dropped the phone when she heard Tony's loud cries. She ran into the kitchen.

"Oh, Tony!" she cried. She grabbed a dish towel and began softly wiping the hot soup off Tony. She felt sick as she saw how badly burned he was.

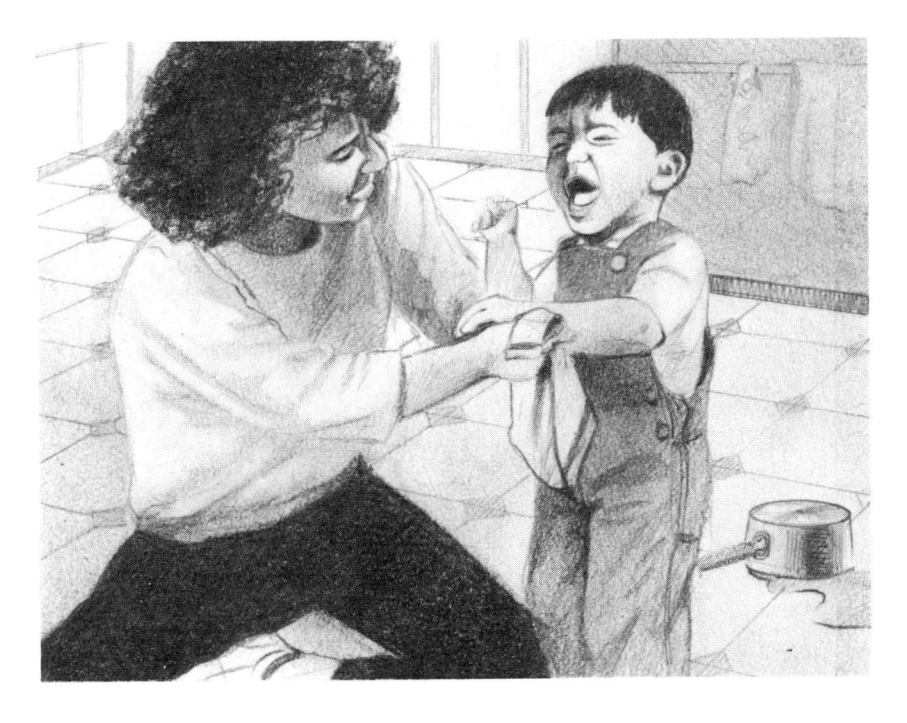

What should I do? Maria thought.

She picked Tony up and ran to the front door.

I hope Josie's home, she thought as she opened the door.

"Josie," Maria shouted up the stairs. "Josie, can you come down? Tony's hurt!"

"I'm coming," Josie called as she started down the stairs.

"Oh, Josie, what should I do?" Maria was crying. "Tony's badly burned."

"Let's call 911," Josie said, picking up the phone. "They'll send help quickly."

Josie dialed 911.

"A two-year-old has been badly burned," she told the operator. "He pulled a pot of hot soup off the stove onto himself." Then she gave the operator Maria's address.

"Is there anything we can do while we're waiting for the emergency team to get here?" Josie asked.

"They'll be there very soon," the operator told her. "But you can give the child water to drink.

Let him lie down. Don't put anything on the burns. If he's cold, cover him with a clean sheet. Don't let a blanket touch the burns."

Does your area have 911 emergency service? If not, you can dial 0 for the operator in an emergency.

Chapter 2   **Help Arrives**

Very soon, two people from the Emergency Medical Service knocked on Maria's door.

"I'm Marge," the woman said. "This is Steve. We understand that a child has been burned."

"Yes," Maria told them. "My son, Tony. I'm glad you came so quickly. I think he's burned very badly."

Marge and Steve looked at Tony's burns.

"We need to take Tony to the hospital," Marge told Maria. "I don't know if he'll have to stay overnight or not. You can ride in the ambulance with us."

"I'll watch for Roberto after school," Josie told Maria.

"Thanks," Maria told her friend. She followed the others to the ambulance.

On the way to the hospital, Maria began to cry.

"I always watch Tony so carefully," she said. "I was just on the phone a minute. I didn't see him go near the stove. I think he smelled the soup cooking and wanted to see what was in the pan."

"Children move quickly," Marge said. "And they are very curious. If pot handles are turned toward the middle of the stove, children can't grab them. And if you use the back burner, children can't reach the pot."

"Try not to worry too much," Steve said. "Dr. Williams will treat Tony at the hospital. I just phoned ahead. She'll be waiting for him when we get there. She knows a lot about burns. Tony's burns are bad, but I think he's going to be all right."

Maria held Tony's hand in hers.

"Mommy's so sorry, darling," she whispered.

Chapter 3   At the Hospital

Dr. Williams was waiting for Tony when they got to the hospital. While the doctor was treating him, Maria talked with a nurse.

"It's hard to watch children every minute," the nurse said. "And it's hard to think of all the ways they can get hurt."

"My six-year-old and I have been working on fire safety in our apartment," Maria said. "But I never thought that Tony would get burned by soup on the stove."

Just then Dr. Williams came into the waiting room.

"Mrs. Gonzalez?" she asked. "I'm Dr. Williams. Tony's going to be all right. He has some bad burns. We'll have to keep him in the hospital for a while. We'll take very good care of him. You and your husband can stay with him as much as you want to while he's here."

"I'm glad Tony will be OK," Maria told Dr. Williams. "Ed, my husband, drives a truck. He's away from home a lot. But I want to stay with Tony as much as I can. I have a first grader to look after, too. So I can't stay all the time.

"Will Tony be all right when I'm not here?" Maria asked.

"Oh, yes," Dr. Williams told her. "Parents don't have to stay with their children in the hospital. But you're welcome to be here whenever you can.

"We're getting Tony ready to be taken to his room now," Dr. Williams told Maria. "Why don't you come with me? You can go with Tony to his room."

"Thanks," Maria said, and she began to cry again.

Dr. Williams put her arm around Maria's shoulders.

"You didn't mean for Tony to get hurt," Dr. Williams said. "Right now, you can help Tony a lot by just being with him. You can read to him and play with him. He's a healthy boy. He'll get well fast.

"We have a very good social worker here at the hospital. She can help you find ways to make your home safer for Tony," Dr. Williams added. "I'll ask her to come by and talk with you when you visit Tony tomorrow."

When Dr. Williams and Maria found Tony, he was lying in a big hospital bed. Maria was happy to see that Tony looked much better now. She held his hand and patted his head as a hospital worker rolled him to his room.

The medicine Dr. Williams had given Tony made him sleepy. So Maria just sat by his bed and held his hand.

Maria stayed with Tony until almost eight o'clock. Then she decided it was best for her to go home to be with Roberto. She would come back

to the hospital the next day after Roberto went to school.

"Good night, darling," she said softly, kissing Tony's forehead.

It was very hard for Maria to leave Tony. But the nurses were very nice. She was sure they would take good care of him.

How would you feel if you were Maria?

Chapter 4   **A Look around the House**

After Roberto went to bed that night, Maria began to look for other ways that Tony could hurt himself. She went through each room looking for dangerous things.

By the time Tony comes home, I want this place to be really safe, Maria decided.

In the living room, Maria saw a glass vase on the coffee table.

Tony has never touched this vase, she thought. But one day he might pick it up. If it broke, he could be cut.

She put the glass vase up high on a shelf.

In her bedroom, Maria took the glass bottles off of the dresser. She put them on top of the chest of drawers. Tony was big enough now to reach the top of the dresser. It was safer for these breakable things to be in a higher place.

In the bathroom, Maria found many dangerous things sitting by the sink—medicines, makeup, mouthwash, and other products. Each product's label said *Keep out of reach of children.*

Maria put all of these things into the top drawer of her chest of drawers. She locked the drawer.

Then Maria went into the kitchen. She had already thrown out the old toaster with the bad cord. And the matches were stored safely in a high cabinet. But when Maria looked under the sink, she realized that the kitchen was the most dangerous room of all.

All of the cleaning products were under the sink. Maria began reading the labels on these products. *Warning: Poison. Danger: Keep out of reach of children. Harmful or fatal if swallowed.*

Tony had never opened this cabinet. But he was getting more and more curious about

everything. He liked to open the low drawer where Maria kept the extra dish towels. He could open the drawer where she kept the forks and spoons. Already she had moved the sharp knives from that drawer to a high shelf out of Tony's reach.

What if Tony opened this cabinet under the sink? she thought. What if he spilled these products on himself? Or sprayed them in his eyes? Or put them in his mouth?

One by one Maria took all of her cleaning products and put them on a high shelf.

Then Maria sat down to rest.

I guess it's time to get rid of this chair with the wobbly leg! she decided. My! I didn't realize how many dangers there were in this house!

Some homes do not have a high shelf or safe storage area for cleaning products. For this reason, people can buy safety bars. These bars will childproof the cupboards that hold dangerous products.

Does your home have any of the dangers that Maria found in her home?

Can you think of any dangers that Maria forgot to look for?

Maria looked mostly for things that were dangerous for a two-year-old. Which dangers that Maria found could also harm an older child?

Do a safety check of your own home. Make a list of the dangers that you find.

- Which dangers can you fix yourself?
- Which dangers must be fixed by your landlord or another repair person?

Chapter 5   The List

The next morning, Maria was up early. As soon as Roberto left for school, she hurried to the hospital. She took Tony's favorite teddy bear and some of his favorite books.

As she went into the children's area, she was surprised by how many children were in the hospital.

Were all these children here last night? she wondered. I guess I was so worried about Tony that I didn't see them, she thought.

Tony slept a lot during the day. Maria talked to other mothers and fathers at the hospital. She met a woman whose son was poisoned when he drank cleaning liquid.

I'm glad I put all my cleaning products on a high shelf last night, Maria thought.

Just before lunchtime, a woman came up to Maria and asked, "Are you Mrs. Gonzalez?"

"Yes," Maria told her. "I'm Tony's mother."

"I'm Rosa, the hospital's social worker," the woman said. "I understand that Tony is doing very well."

"Yes," Maria said. "His burns could have been a lot worse."

"Many, many children are hurt in accidents at home," Rosa said. "Parents just can't be too careful. It's hard to think of all the ways that children can get hurt at home."

"I know," said Maria. "Last night, I went through my whole apartment looking for ways that Tony could get hurt. I always thought our home was safe for little children. But I was surprised at how many dangerous things I found!"

Rosa nodded.

"We see so many children here who have had accidents at home," she said. "We've made a list of things parents can check to be sure their home is safe for children. I'd like to give you a copy of the list."

"Thank you," Maria said. "I wish I'd had this before Tony got burned."

After Rosa left, Maria looked at the list. She was surprised at how long it was. As she read the list, she found the things she already had done at her apartment. But she also found many more things she'd never even thought about.

15 Ways to Make Your Home Safer

1. Put all breakable things out of children's reach.

2. Install smoke detectors on each level of your home, and in the hallway near sleeping areas. Test the batteries each month.

3. Remove or repair any chairs or tables that are wobbly, unstable, breakable, or have sharp corners.

4. Remove any peeling paint. Some paint contains lead, which can poison children if they eat it.

5. Check for splinters and loose nails. Keep everything in your home in good repair.

6. Put electric appliances where the cords are out of children's reach, and where they won't need extension cords.

7. Replace electric cords that are broken or frayed.

8. Never overload electric outlets by having too many cords plugged in.

9. Cover unused electric outlets with safety plugs.

10. Keep all medicines, toiletries such as shampoo and lotion, and household cleansers in their original containers. Store them away from food and out of children's reach.

11. Never use thin plastic bags around children for any purpose.

12. Set your water heater at *normal* to prevent scalding.

13. Be sure there is no way for children to lock themselves in the bathroom.

14. Keep garbage cans where children cannot get into them.

15. Keep your yard free of such things as rusty nails and broken glass.

Chapter 6   **Childproofing the Apartment**

At home that night, Maria read the safety list again. Then she went through the whole apartment, checking everything on the list.

There were two smoke detectors in the apartment. Maria checked the batteries in both of them. Both batteries were fine.

In the living room, Maria looked at the sharp corners on the coffee table. Tony could cut himself badly if he fell on one of these corners, she thought. We'd better put this table in a closet until he's older. She unscrewed the table's legs and carried it to the bedroom closet.

The paint in the boys' room was peeling in several places. Maria didn't know if it contained lead or not, but she didn't want to take a chance. I'll call the landlord, she decided. He should scrape the old paint off and repaint this room.

Maria also checked the apartment for splinters and loose nails while she was looking around for peeling paint.

The radio beside Maria's bed was plugged into an extension cord. She often had to tell Tony not to play with the cord. Better put the radio

someplace else, Maria thought. I think it will do fine on the high chest of drawers—if I tuck the cord behind the chest.

Maria checked all the electric cords to be sure they were in good condition. Then she checked all the outlets in the apartment. Most outlets had only one cord plugged into them.

One outlet in the living room had four cords plugged into an adapter. If all of these things are turned on at one time, that would probably overload the outlet, Maria thought. She looked around for a way to use other outlets in the room.

I've never seen a safety plug, Maria thought as she looked at number nine on the list. I'll have to ask about them at the hardware store. She wrote *safety plugs* on her shopping list.

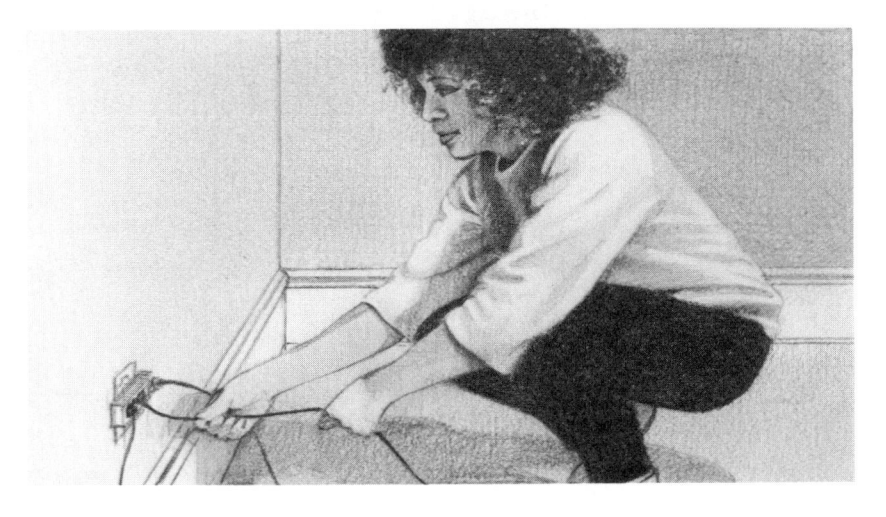

Maria was glad she had already put the medicines, toiletries, and cleaning products out of Tony's reach. She checked the kitchen for thin plastic bags. She looked at the dial on the water heater to be sure it wasn't set too hot.

Then Maria looked at the hook on the bathroom door. It's low enough that Tony could fasten it, she thought. But what if he couldn't get it open again? She moved the hook higher on the door.

Maria's apartment building used a Dumpster, so there were no garbage cans outside for children to get into. Maria looked at the small garbage can in the kitchen. Tony could get into that easily, she thought. I guess I could use a paper bag and put it up on the washing machine. I'd have to carry it out more often, but that's OK. I want to be sure Tony is safe.

The last place on the list was the yard. The apartment building didn't have much of a yard. But there were a lot of empty bottles and cans and other trash on the sidewalk in front of the building.

Maria decided to ask her friend Josie and some of the other neighbors to help clean up around the building. Then all the neighborhood

children would have a safer place to play. The neighborhood would look better, too, Maria thought.

By the time Maria finished childproofing her apartment, she was very tired. Before she went to bed, she looked in on Roberto, who was already fast asleep. I'm so glad he never had a bad accident, she thought. And I don't want Tony to ever get hurt again.

Maria took the safety list and taped it to the refrigerator door. This apartment is a safe place now, she told herself. And I'm going to keep it that way.

Think about the Story

1. Has your child ever had a bad accident? What did you do? Where did you get help?

2. Would your home pass a safety check based on Maria's safety list? What changes would you have to make so that it would pass?

3. Can you think of more safety tips to add to Maria's safety list?

   Make a list of these.

Ideas from the Story

Children are naturally active and curious. It is good for them to explore the world around them. Adults can help children by making their world as safe as possible.

Children should not have to be told *Don't touch that!* all the time. If there is something harmful where the child lives or plays, it should be removed.

Keeping a house or an apartment safe for children takes time and effort. Parents should make a safety check every day.

Some important things to watch out for:

- breakable things that might cut children
- furniture or electric appliances in bad condition
- things that children can choke on
- poisonous products

The time it takes to make your home safe is time well spent.

End of Parent's Story